Blessing

Teresa K

MW00780956

Endorsement

The holiness of God is love that burns so intensely that it consumes all that is not love into itself. Teresa has painted word picture after word picture that beckon us to discover that such love lives within us, revealing the infinite value of the child as can only be found in the infinite heart of their creator.

-Mark and Risa Evans
Founders of Hope Preserved: a Christian counseling ministry for SRA survivors

REDEFINED

Who You Are In Christ

Teresa Burleson

Redefined: Who You Are In Christ

Unless otherwise indicated, all Scripture quotations are taken from the *New American Standard Bible*, Copyright 1960, 1971, 1977, 1995 by The Lockman Foundation. Used by permission. All rights reserved.

Scriptures marked KJV are taken from the King James Version, public domain.

Scripture quotations marked NKJV are taken from the *New King James Version*. Copyright 1982 by Thomas Nelson, Inc. Used by permission. All rights reserved.

Cover and interior design by Marji Laine
Published by:

Roaring Lambs Publishing
17110 Dallas Parkway, Suite 260
Dallas, TX 75248

Printed in the United States of America

Dedication

For Dempsy Burleson
(1953-2020).

Thanks for marrying me.
Thanks for teaching me that God is God.

Table of Contents

Teresa Burleson

Labeled

Like a straitjacket, a label confines, restricts, and and holds me back from being all God means me to be. So many times, the labels others place on me just don't fit. Day by day, I am barraged by the enemy of my soul telling me I am unworthy, unwanted and unacceptable. He calls me an orphan, a victim, a nobody.

So who will I believe? Where can I go to find the truth about myself? My Maker, the One who knows everything about me, including why He made me, has given me His Word. Listening to what He says, I find my purpose even in a world that tells me I have no meaning, and no purpose.

Who will I let define me this day? Can I be redefined? I have the power to choose. I decide who will tell me who I am. In this 31-day devotional journey, I explore exactly who I am in Christ according to the Word of God. I invite you to come along. Because my Father is your Father. And what He is saying about me, He is saying about you. He has told us who we are.

Dear Father of us all,
*   Thank You that You have given us Your Word. Your Word is the truth. And You alone tell us the truth about ourselves. Thank You that our worth, our value, and our identity are in You alone.*

Redefined

How quickly I sink
Beneath the frown
Of those who deem me
Of no value,
A nobody.
Remind me again,
You who cannot lie,
That I am Yours.
You saw me
From the beginning,
And You alone
May give me my name.
I am handcrafted,
Known through and through,
Partaker of Your nature.
You who cannot lie
Have told me
Who I am.

Teresa Burleson

I Am His Image Bearer

God created man in His own image;
in the image of God He created him;
male and female He created them.
Genesis 1:27

An image represents something else. Whatever the medium they use, artists create an image. They aim to somehow capture the essence of the original. The first chapter of Genesis tells me that I am an image, stamped with the likeness of God Himself.

But what does it mean to bear the image of the Almighty, the Maker of the whole universe? He is the Creator. I am the creature. He is infinite. I am finite. He is holy. I am sinful and flawed. Yes, I am broken by the fall. Yet the fact remains he chose to create me as a unique expression of who He is. It is in my DNA. This is why I can feel, think, love, choose, will, dream, and (in my own limited way) create. As His image bearer, I show Him to the world around me. How well will I reflect Him this day?

Maker of all things,

You have made me in Your own likeness. What a privilege and responsibility to bear Your image! May I represent You well to those around me. May they see more of You and less of me.

Image Bearer

Formed by His finger,
One of a kind,
Here for a reason,
Plucked from the mire,
Now wearing white,

Defaced likeness,
Now being restored,
Immortal,
Crafted by the Holy,

I am an image bearer.

Teresa Burleson

I Am His Child

"And I will be a father to you,
And you shall be sons and daughters to Me,"
says the Lord Almighty.
II Cor. 6:18

See how great a love the Father has bestowed on us,
that we should be called children of God; and such we are.
I John 3:1

The Jews claimed to know the One True God. They were His chosen people. However, they did not know Him as Father. When Jesus dared to call God His Father, the Pharisees considered it blasphemy. They were outraged and ready to put Him to death.

Along with addressing God as His Father, Jesus made a way for me to know Him as my Father. Because of what the Son did on the cross, I, too, can call God my Abba Father.

Not only is God my Father, He is the best possible Father. He loves me not because of anything I do or don't do, but simply because I am His. He chooses to share His divine nature with me. Just as children take their father's last name, so God allows me to take His Name with me everywhere I go. Only His Name is above all other names.

Unlike many earthly fathers, my Heavenly Father is ever faithful to meet my needs and give me the training and discipline He sees that I need to grow in righteousness. Born in sin and bent on rebellion, I was estranged from God. But now, covered by the blood of Jesus, I can draw near to God, not as a servant cringing in fear, but as a little child climbing into her daddy's lap. I am no longer an orphan. I belong. I have a Father.

Heavenly Father,
    Thank You for claiming me and caring for me as Your own child. Thank You for desiring that kind of relationship with me. Thank You for being such a wonderful Father.

Child Of The Father

I am fire-purged,
Grace-fashioned,
Love-enfolded.

I am overshadowed,
Much delivered,
Spirit-borne.

I am sorely tested,
Not forsaken,
Footsore--but still climbing.

I am a found sheep,
Emerging butterfly.
I am my Father's child.

A Fierce Embrace

On a day
Like no other,
The Light found me.
The Light immersed me,
Purging,
Exposing,
Enfolding me.
And in that embrace,
I was fathered.
I was quickened.
Darkness was evicted.
The Light found me.

I Am His Sheep

We are His people and the sheep of His pasture.
Psalm 100:3

The Lord is my shepherd, I shall not want.
Psalm 23:1

I am the good Shepherd;
the good shepherd lays down his life for the sheep.
John 10:11

With little intelligence or ability to take care of themselves, sheep are defenseless against predators and prone to stray. They need a shepherd. In the time of Jesus, a group of shepherds would all bring their flocks to a large central pen for safekeeping at night. All of the shepherds except for one would go home for the night. The one remaining would lay down on the ground with his body across the only way into the sheepfold. Any thieves, whether two-footed or four-footed, would literally have to get across his dead body to get to the sheep.

I, too, need a shepherd. I have an enemy more vicious and cunning than any wolf. He is relentless. He comes only to kill, steal, and destroy (John 10:10). But Jesus, the best possible Shepherd, has interposed his own body between me and certain doom. I am rescued. He laid down His life for a feeble and foolish stray like me. Will He not also give me the green pastures and still waters I need? He is my Shepherd. I shall not want.

Dear Lord Jesus,

You are the Good Shepherd. Thank You for laying down Your life for the sheep. I cannot thank You enough. Help me to follow Your leading and trust You to give me all the pastures and still waters I need for this day. You are my Shepherd. I shall not lack.

Rescued

This Shepherd is found
Not in stained glass
But in pursuit
Of every stray.
Sooner or later
We find ourselves
At the bottom
Of the crevice.
There we lie
With no way out.
But He can hear
Our faintest bleat.
However deep
The ravine may be,
However besmirched
We may be,
He comes at once.
Nothing deters Him.
Gently He pulls us
From the brambles
And puts us
On the only shoulders
That can bear
The weight of us all.

Teresa Burleson

I Am A New Creation

*Therefore if anyone is in Christ, he is a new creature; the old
things passed away; behold new things have come.*
II Corinthians 5:17

First it devours every green thing it can find. Then
the furry wriggler hangs from a twig and entombs
itself. But out of what seems like death, comes life.
A few weeks later, something entirely new,
something with wings will emerge.

Even though it was on the inside, not the
outside, just as wondrous a change happened in my
life. Like the creature that came out of the chrysalis,
I am not who I was.

Born in sin, I was by nature a child of wrath
(Eph. 2:3). But on October 31, 1971, at a high school
youth retreat in the Santa Cruz mountains, I came

face to face with Jesus. Just as soon as I received Him, I received power to become a child of God (John 1:12). He gave me a new nature. Then I began being made like my Maker. Because of what occurred that day, I have a new DNA, a new destination, and a new destiny. The past no longer defines me. I have passed from death into life. He who makes all things new now lives in me.

Dear Lord,

I give You praise for being the One who makes all things new. Thank You for making me a new creation. Thank You that I can walk in newness of life this day.

Metamorphosis

Held captive
In this tiny prison,
I am a pupa
Slowly morphing
Into a creature
Ready to take flight
On newly won wings,
Reflecting the splendor
Of that face
I shall someday see.

Teresa Burleson

I Am The Clay

But now, O Lord, You are our Father,
we are the clay, and You, our potter;
and all of us are the work of Your hand.
Isaiah 64:8

Unlike the clay taken from the ground, I can talk back to my Potter. I can, and often do resist Him. I question Him. Sometimes I even try to get off the potter's wheel! But like the clay that comes from the ground, I am nothing until His hands shape me. Only He understands why I was made and how to make me into a masterpiece, a vessel of honor (II Tim. 2:20-21). He sees what I cannot. He sees the finished product. The real question is will I trust the Potter? Will I trust Him when it takes so long on the potter's wheel? Will I trust Him even in the kiln?

I can argue with my Maker. I can be stubborn in His hands and resist His will. Or I can let Him make me into the work of art He saw from the beginning. The choice is mine.

Master Potter,

Thank You that You know what You are doing. Thank You for loving me enough to shape me into a vessel of honor. Even when it hurts, even when I tire of the process, Lord, help me to trust You. Help me to say yes to Your expert shaping. May I say yes to You even this day.

The Craftsman

Change comes on the inside
As the stubborn clay says yes
To that skillful hand,
Yes to His strange ways,
Yes to His slow shaping,
Yes to Him who alone
Knows how to craft a soul.

Teresa Burleson

I Am Light

You are the light of the world.
A city set on a hill cannot be hidden.
Matthew 5:14

Does one small light even matter? During WWII blackouts, civilians were not allowed to light even a match, use a flashlight, or smoke a cigarette out in the open or near a window.

Any light at all might help enemy bombers find their targets. The darkness was no match for even a tiny light.

One of light's amazing properties is that it disperses or scatters darkness. It exposes everything that is hidden. Without it, I grope around trying to find my way. I stumble and don't even know what I am stumbling over.

In the spiritual realm, as in the natural, darkness

flees before light. Jesus is the Light and He has come to stay (John 8:12) and there is no darkness in Him (I John 1:5). And because He is in me, His light shines in and through me. I am a child of light. That is my new identity (Ephesians 5:8). As I allow Him to expose the darkness in me and as I draw closer to His radiance, I reflect more of His light to other people.

Sometimes I wonder if my tiny, borrowed light can make any difference. The enemy tries to tell me no one sees or cares anyway. So I might as well hide it under a bushel. But if I put my lamp on whatever lampstand I am given and let my light shine wherever I am, others will see and they will glorify the Father (Matt. 5:15-16).

Dear Jesus,

You have come to stay and darkness flees before You. Cast out the darkness in me. Help me to let go of any secret sin. I ask You to shine in me and through me, brighter and brighter, until the perfect Day. Keep me walking in the Light.

Expose

The Light will find us out.
We cannot hide.
We cannot escape
His fearsome brightness.
He looks on us,
Exposing darkness,
Consuming the impure,
Until we become
Bearers of the Light.

Teresa Burleson

I Am Seated In Heavenly Places

But God, being rich in mercy,
because of His great love with which He loved us,
even when we were dead in our transgressions,
made us alive together with Christ
(by grace you have been saved)
and raised us up with Him
in the heavenly places in Christ Jesus.
Ephesians 2:4-6

The INS may never deport me, but I am an alien (I Peter 2:11). I am in the world but not of the world (John 17:16). My citizenship is in heaven (Phil. 3:20).

I have a new permanent address and the altitude is mind boggling. It is all a matter of location. Since I am in Christ and He is in me, His location is also my location. And He is seated at the right hand of the Father. That means I have full access to the Ruler of the whole universe. There is no higher authority. Even now, He is waiting to do through me what only He can do. He is unstoppable.

But will I let Him work through me? I must decide. Will I focus on the situation? Will I believe the circumstances? Or will I take Him at His Word? Will I believe what He says and stake my life on it? Will I see myself as a victim, or as victorious in Him? Kingdom authority is mine. Now I want to learn to walk in it. The choice is mine. Things are not what they appear. No matter how bleak or chaotic my outward situation may look this day, I am seated with Him.

Lord Jesus,

You are Lord of all. Thank You that I am in You and You are in me. Thank You for giving me authority in Your Name. Help me to walk in it this day. Thank You that I am no longer a victim. Thank You that I am seated with You in heavenly places.

I Am Salt

You are the salt of the earth;
but if the salt has become tasteless,
how can it be made salty again?
It is no longer good for anything
except to be thrown out and trampled under foot by men.
Matthew 5:13

Salt makes a difference. A nobleman once passed through a village in Cornwall, England. Finding nowhere to buy himself some liquor, he became irate. He complained to a villager about it. The man replied, "My Lord, something over a hundred years ago, a man named John Wesley came to these parts." And that was all he said.[i]

John Wesley was salt. He was a difference maker. He made a difference in his generation. In the same way, countless other believers, male and female, young and old, from all walks of life, have been difference makers.

Before refrigeration, salt was a crucial ingredient in food. It kept meat from spoiling. Rotting food is an apt picture of the world around me. It needs a preservative! I don't have to look very far to see the corruption. Every time I get on the internet or go somewhere like Wal-Mart, the evidence bombards me. The moral decay is rampant. Who will stand against it and act as a preservative? Who else will be salt, if not believers who have Christ living in them? So I ask myself what kind of impact my actions and words are having on those around me. Am I making a difference? Am I being salt?

Oh, Lord Jesus,
Please help me to make a difference where I am. I want to be a difference maker in my generation. Live Your life through me. Please don't let me lose my saltiness.

I Am Found

*For the Son of Man has come to seek
and to save that which was lost.*
Luke 19:10

The Ruler of everything visited this planet. When we were helpless and hopeless, He chose to make a personal appearance. So began the ultimate search and rescue mission. Jesus met sinners right where they were. He did whatever it took to confront them with the truth and bring them back to the Father. Whether it was the despised Samaritan woman at the well, Matthew at the tax booth, the Gadarene demoniac shrieking among the tombs, or Zaccheus hiding in the sycamore tree, Jesus saw their need and sought them out.

At the age of 17, I didn't even know I was lost. I had a respectable and religious persona that I presented to the world. I looked pretty good on the outside. Hey, I was usually the one who answered the questions in Sunday School class. But on the inside, it was a different story. I was a child of wrath (Ephesians 2:3), estranged from God and on my way to perdition. In His mercy, God wooed and drew me to Himself. Then at just the right time, He brought someone across my path who knew what to say, when I was ready to hear it. When I was without hope and helpless to save myself, Jesus rescued me. I once was lost but now am found. And nothing has ever been the same.

My Rescuer,

You left Heaven to seek and save me. Thank You so much. May I never forget what You saved me from and all You saved me for.

I Am His Vessel

But we have this treasure in earthen vessels, so that the surpassing greatness of the power will be of God and not from ourselves.
II Corinthians 4:7

Now in a large house there are not only gold and silver vessels, but also vessels of wood and of earthenware, and some to honor and some to dishonor.
II Tim. 2:20

On the outside, an exquisite Greek amphora kept in a museum and an ordinary clay pot may look very different. But they are both empty containers. A vessel is only useful when it is filled. Its sole purpose is to hold something.

I, too, am an empty vessel in need of filling. I am but dust. I am nothing until the Holy Spirit fills me with Himself. So what are the requirements for being filled? There are only two. If I am looking for something to drink coffee from, I'm probably not going to choose the jar already full of pickles. And I'm probably not going to choose the dirty mug in the sink. I want something that is both empty and clean.

If I really want God to fill me and use me, I must make room in my heart for Him. I must come empty of self. That means coming with no agenda of my own and waiting on Him for His agenda, as well as confessing and repenting of any known sin and receiving His forgiveness (I John 1:9). Once I realize my need for Him and come with a clean heart, the Spirit fills me. I become useable.

God seeks empty containers waiting to be filled. He is looking for someone He can work through, anyone willing to be used. What about me? Am I ready for His use? What about today?

Holy Spirit,
I desperately need Your cleansing and filling. Please fall afresh on me. Work in me as only You can until I am a vessel of honor. Help me to remember that You are the treasure. I am only the container.

I Am The Righteousness Of God In Christ Jesus

He made Him who knew no sin to be sin on our behalf, so that
we might become the righteousness of God in Him.
II Corinthians 5:21

After seeing the finger of God nine times, Pharoah still hardened his heart. One more plague remained. And it was the worst. The Lord was about to strike the firstborn of Egypt, man and beast. But first, the Israelites were instructed to take a lamb for each household, kill it at twilight and roast it to eat. They were also to dip a hyssop branch in some of the blood and smear it on the doorposts and lintels of all their houses. That night the Angel of Death passed through the whole land. Wherever he saw the blood over the door, he passed by that house. The firstborn of Israel were spared.

Like those doorposts, I am marked with the blood. God is too holy to look on sin. But now when He looks at me, He doesn't see my utter sinfulness. He sees only the blood of His dear Son. Jesus is my covering, my substitute, my Passover Lamb. He is my righteousness. Mine is as filthy rags (Is. 64:6). But now I have a new wardrobe. Thank God, I stand before Him dressed in His sinless perfection.

Lord Jesus,

You did it all on the cross. Thank You for being my covering, my righteousness, my Advocate with the Father. Thank You that there is power in Your Blood.

Passover

Yahweh has written
With hyssop
Over my door-posts.
This graffiti
Cannot be expunged.
It forever marks me
As His own.
The Perfect is slain
For the imperfect.
The books are balanced.
The leper is made clean.
The destroyer departs
Leaving me untouched.
I am bought with a price.

Teresa Burleson

I Am Dead To Sin
I Am Alive To God

But God, being rich in mercy,
because of His great love with which He loved us,
even when we were dead in our transgressions,
made us alive together with Christ.
Ephesians 2:4-5

They threw her to the ground at His feet. She hid her face in her hands. They had known just where to find her. Of course, they let the man go, even though the law stipulated that both should be stoned. The One they brought her to said nothing. Slowly He stooped down and began writing in the sand. Finally, He said, "Let the one who is without sin, throw the first stone." Their mouths closed. One by one, they dropped their stones and left. When they were gone, He helped her to her feet. His gaze was penetrating but kind. She saw no accusation. Then she knew. The only One there without sin refused to join her accusers. He was her champion.

Every bit as guilty as the woman caught in adultery, I, too, was accused by the enemy and condemned to die. I was under a death sentence. I was, in fact, spiritually dead. I, too, found Jesus to be my champion. Instead of accusing me, He took the punishment for me.

When I was baptized into Christ, I was actually crucified along with Him. The old me died. In the same way, I now partake in His resurrection. Because He lives in me, I can say no to sin. It rules me no longer. I can choose Life.

My Champion,

When I was dead in sin, You made me alive together with You. Today I will walk with You. Today I will choose Life. I present my members to You as instruments of righteousness.

No Condemnation

(John 8:1-11)

There was no stoning
That day.
Her sentence was commuted
by the One
Without sin.
They saw only her guilt
And a chance
To trap Him.
He saw a soul
Waiting to be salvaged.
He spoke the word
And her nightmare ended.
Her life began.

Final Argument

The gavel falls.
There is no question
About the verdict.
There is no question
About what I deserve,
Except my only Defense
Arrives just in time.
One glimpse
Of that nail-scarred wrist
Leaves the prosecutor
Without a word.
The charges are dropped.
The penalty is paid.
And though I am guilty
As can be,
The Judge Himself
Finds me faultless.

I Am Redeemed

But now, thus says the Lord your Creator, O Jacob,
And He who formed you, O Israel,
do not fear for I have redeemed you;
I have called you by name, you are mine!
Isaiah 43:1

Bedraggled and broken, she had nowhere to hide. Gomer was on the auction block waiting to be sold to the highest bidder. I wonder what she felt when the buyer turned out to be the man she had wronged most, her husband, the prophet Hosea. Like Gomer, I have wronged the One who has loved me most. I have been unfaithful to the One who has given me everything, the One who has never stopped seeking me. Just like Gomer, I have left Him for other lovers. I was just another victim of the ultimate human trafficker. And like Hosea, Jesus bought me back.

In this world, we determine something's worth

by how much money it takes to purchase it. Unlike Gomer, who was bought back with only fifteen pieces of silver, I have been redeemed with the lifeblood of God Himself. There is no way to measure what it cost Him. Surely, He paid King's ransom for my soul. I am bought with a price (I Cor. 6:20).

My Dear Redeemer,

Thank You for buying me back from sin's slave market and certain death. Thank You that You paid it all. Thank You that Your blood will never lose its power.

Gomer Speaks

Many times
This heart has played
The harlot.
All too soon,
My choices
Became my shackles.
But he was waiting
At the auction block.
Instead of the lashes
I deserved,
I felt his own cloak
Enfolding me,
Covering all my shame.
I cannot explain
Such a love.
How can you measure
The cost of such a love?
I only know
The past is gone.
The bride is reclaimed.

Teresa Burleson

I Am Chosen

You who I have taken from the ends of the earth,
and called from its remotest parts and said to you,
"You are my servant, I have chosen you and not rejected you.
Isaiah 41:9

Someone who is 4'8" doesn't always get a lot of respect. I know. I was always the smallest in my class. I remember not getting chosen for whatever sport we were playing. I remember not being picked as a cheerleader. I remember not being asked to dance. I knew the feeling of being overlooked and passed by. I learned early that most people tend to judge by outward appearance.

But when God looks at me, He sees exactly what He has placed on the inside (I Samuel 16:7). He sees my purpose, the special task I was born to do, that no one else can do in exactly the same way.

Even with all my limitations, all my lack of faith and just plain orneriness, He still chooses to work through me and partner with me. His strength is made perfect in my weakness (II Cor. 12:9). He has chosen to make even me a trophy for His grace. I am here for a reason. God has an assignment for me to fulfill. And everyday, whether I realize it or not, I am deciding if I will accept the assignment. The choice is mine. May I accept the assignment I am given today. Whatever people say or don't say about me, may I remember that God calls me chosen.

Dear God,

It is so good to know You have chosen me and not rejected me. I praise Your Name. Thank You for choosing to work through all my quirks and frailties. You are God and there is no limit to what You can do in or through me.

Hand Picked

He has a way of choosing
The overlooked.
He has a way of using
The unlikely,
The unlovely,
The unqualified,
The unimpressive.
The All-seeing views
Each of us
Just as we are.
And those who will be
Satisfied
With nothing less
Than His dear Presence,
Will be hand picked.

Teresa Burleson

I Am Accepted

To the praise of the glory of His grace,
through which he hath made us accepted in the Beloved.
Ephesians 1:6 KJV

It leaves scars when a girl finds out her mother wanted a son instead of a daughter. It leaves scars that can last a lifetime.

Is there healing for that kind of pain? Is there anyone or anything that can fill the emptiness? In my life, God used my deepest pain to woo me and draw me to Himself. I was looking for acceptance and I found it in the One who made me and knows all about me and accepts me just the way I am. It was revolutionary. When others make me feel unaccepted, I can turn to the One who said in John 6:37, that He will never cast out the one who comes to Him.

Because He declares me acceptable, I can enjoy just being who He made me to be. And when I find my acceptance and self worth in Him, it frees me to love other people even as I am loved.

Oh, God,

You are Perfect Love. Thank You for accepting me just as I am. Thank You for not casting me away or giving up on me. Thank You that Your Love for me is not based on my performance.

Please help me to grow in my acceptance of other people.

I Am Adopted

*He predestined us to adoption as sons through Jesus Christ to
Himself, according to the kind intention of His will.*
Ephesians 1:5

*And not only this, but also we ourselves;
having the first fruits of the Spirit,
even we ourselves groan within ourselves,
waiting eagerly for our adoption as sons,
the redemption of our body.*
Romans 8:23

Adoption means a child is chosen. There is nothing second class about it. My husband and I adopted two children from foreign countries, South Korea and Guatemala. We chose them and earnestly prayed for them during the seemingly interminable process. Finally, they were placed in our home. They became ours in every sense of the word. Two orphans now belonged to a family. They had the same legal rights, including the right to inherit, as any biological child.

Teresa Burleson

I, too, am adopted into the family of God. I am no longer an orphan. Jesus Himself claims me as kin. He is my elder brother and someday I will inherit all things along with Him. When our children were placed in our home, that was not the end of the process. An adoption has to be finalized. Likewise, I have the Spirit of Adoption living inside me in the here and now. Over and over, He lets me know that God is my Father and I am His child. And someday, when I leave this body behind, He will give me a resurrection body like His. On that day, my adoption will be finalized.

Abba Father,
Thank You for adopting me, choosing me and including me in Your family circle. Thank You that I belong. Thank You for giving me the Spirit of Adoption to constantly remind me that I am Yours. May I hear what the Spirit is whispering to me this day.

Relationship

Standing before Him,
I see in His hand
Not a report card,
Scoreboard
Or bank account
But a decree of adoption.

Teresa Burleson

I Am His Friend

You are my friends If you do what I command you.
No longer do I call you slaves,
for the slave does not know what his master is doing;
but I have called you friends,
for all things that I have heard from My Father
I have made known to you.
John 15:14-15

My husband of 41 years died of brain cancer on Feb. 12, 2020. As he was dying, God whispered to me, "You're not losing your best friend."

Since then, it has been very difficult, even for an extreme introvert like me, to live by myself. But a little at a time, without anyone else to depend on, I have been discovering the truth of what the Lord said. He is the friend who sticks closer than a brother (Prov. 18:24). As Joseph Scriven wrote in his enduring hymn, it is my "privilege to carry everything to Him in prayer."

But a friendship always has two sides. So I

wonder, what kind of friend am I to Him? In John 15:14, Jesus says that I show my friendship to Him by how well I obey His commands.

Two friends are free to confide in or share secrets with each other. I can safely share my heart with Him, but how much can the Lord trust me with His secrets, His counsel? In the Revised Standard Version, Psalm 25:14 says, "The friendship of the lord is for those who fear him, and he makes known to them His covenant." To fear the Lord is to obey Him. I want to walk in a healthy fear of the Lord so He can trust me with His secrets and His counsel. I want to be a better friend.

Lord Jesus,

What a friend I have in You! Thank You for being my best friend in every season of my life. It is a wonderful privilege to be Your servant, but You have even called me friend. Please help me to be a better friend to You. Help me to want to obey You. Forgive me for ever taking a friendship with You lightly.

I Am The Branch

I am the vine, you are the branches;
he who abides in Me and I in him, he bears much fruit,
for apart from Me you can do nothing.
John 15:5

You did not choose Me but I chose you,
and appointed you that you would go and bear fruit,
and that your fruit would remain,
so that whatever you ask of the Father in My name He may
give to you.
John 15:16

A shapely red oak tree graces my front yard. Most of the branches are healthy and leafy. But a few are not. For whatever reason, they have not received the nutrients they need. With no life in them, no leaves, they are fit only for the fire.

Just as the branches draw their life from the tree, so I must draw my life from Jesus. He is my life. So how do I abide in Him? First, I recognize my constant need for Him. Then I feed on His Word and converse with Him throughout the day. As I abide in this close, vital union with Him, His sap flows through me and makes me fruitful. Like any good gardener who wants much fruit, God takes out the pruning sheers when needed. Whether it involves a possession, finances, health, or a relationship, pruning is never fun. I may hate the process, but the Vinedresser knows just what is necessary for my maximum fruitfulness. As I remain daily in the Vine, He is able to give the increase. He alone sustains me and keeps me green even in the driest times. Because He lives in me, I am evergreen (Psalm 92:14).

Dear Jesus,

You are the Vine. I am the branch. Help me remember You are my life. And apart from You I can do nothing. Let Your sap rise in me. Keep me abiding in You. Thank You that You give the increase. Thank You that Love holds the pruning sheers.

The Vinedresser

In His vineyard
There is no waste.
In His vineyard
There is no loss.
So tenderly
We are tended
Until each grape is ready
For the winepress,
Until we are His sweet wine
Poured out for the thirsty.

Teresa Burleson

The Alternative

Pruning sheers are
Not my choice.
Oh, that the pain would end!
I prefer pruning,
Though,
And fruit bearing
To becoming dead wood
Fit only for the fire

I Am Sent In His Name

All authority has been given to Me
in heaven and on earth.
Go therefore and make disciples of all the nations, baptizing
them in the name of the Father and the Son
and the Holy Spirit.
Matthew 28:18-19

Several times, I worked door to door as a Census taker. I had to wear an official badge letting people know I really was an employee of the U.S. Census Bureau. Because of that badge, people would usually give me the information I needed. They knew I was not there on my own authority. I was representing the Census Bureau.

Just as I had the backing of the Federal Government then, so I am now authorized and commissioned by a much higher authority. Jesus Himself sends me out as His witness, His ambassador. Whether I realize it or not, I represent the King everywhere I go. At times, the task is overwhelming. In my own strength, it is impossible. But when I receive power from on High, the Holy Spirit promised by Jesus in Acts 1:8, nothing is impossible. Today, I will go where He sends me, in the knowledge that I bear His Name, the Name above all Names. That is what I call authorized.

Dear Lord Jesus,

You are King of Kings. Give me courage to go anywhere You send me. May I fulfill the assignment in Your power even this day. Thank You for the privilege of bearing Your Name.

I Am Forgiven

Then He said to her,
"Your sins have been forgiven."
Luke 7:48

I still remember the Summer I was 17. For the first and only time, I backpacked in Yosemite with my church youth group. The pack on my back was less than 40 lb. but it sure felt heavier to me.

In John Bunyan's classic, *Pilgrim's Progress*, Christian travels from the City of Destruction to the Celestial City. He, too, is wearing a large pack on his back. The further he goes, the heavier it grows. The miserable pilgrim wonders if there is any way to rid himself of the terrible weight. But just when he can bear it no longer, he reaches the cross. There the pack flies off his back and falls into a hole that suddenly opens in the earth. He never sees it again.

Like Christian, I have known the feeling of being weighed down by sin and guilt. And like him, I found no relief, no remedy until Jesus found me. He is the only solution for my sin problem. As co-equal with God, He has the right to forgive sins. As the Lamb of God, He is the Perfect Sacrifice. As my Advocate, He pleads for me with the Father.

With His last breath, Jesus exclaimed, "It is finished!" He used the same word that was written across tax receipts when they were paid in full. All my many, many sins, past, present, and future are paid for. Because He took my burden, all of it, I can face the journey.

Lord Jesus,
You really did pay it all! I can never thank You enough. May I be quick to forgive others even as You forgive all my sins and cleanse me from all unrighteousness (I John 1:9).

I Am Saved By Grace

*For by grace you have been saved through faith;
and that not of yourselves, it is the gift of God;
not as a result of works, so that no one may boast.*
Ephesians 2:8-9

The Titanic sped to her doom despite six warnings that danger lay ahead. On April 14, 1912, the luxury liner struck an iceberg and began to sink. There were only 20 lifeboats, not enough for the 2,224 passengers. Because the evacuation was poorly managed, many lifeboats were launched before they were filled to capacity. The ship took 2 hours and 40 minutes to sink. All those left on board, approximately 1,490-1,635, perished in one of the worst peacetime maritime disasters on record.[ii]

Like the Titanic, this world is a vessel heading for destruction without the passengers even realizing it. In I John 2:17, the Apostle says this world is passing away along with its lusts. So how can I be saved? There is only one Lifeboat and His Name is Jesus. He is the only way, the one safe place in a world that is surely perishing. Unlike the lifeboats on the Titanic, there is plenty of room. There is room for all who choose Him. Still, I must choose to get on the lifeboat. God has taken the most extreme measures imaginable for me to be saved. But the choice is mine.

I cannot save myself. There is no way I could ever earn it or make myself worthy. But the good news is I don't have to. That is why it is called grace. It is the free gift of God.

Dear Jesus,
   You are the Lifeboat. Thank You for being my one safe place. Thank You that You did it all on the cross. I receive it now.

I Am His Treasured Possession

Now then, if you will indeed obey My voice
and keep my covenant,
then you shall be My own possession among all the peoples,
for all the earth is Mine.
Exodus 19:5

The Lord has today declared you to be His people,
a treasured possession, as He promised you,
and that you should keep all His commandments.
Deuteronomy 26:18

They are magnificent. And they are the property of the Monarch of England. Comprised of 23,578 stones, including the largest clear-cut diamond in the world, the crown jewels of England include all the regalia and vestments used by the Kings and Queens of England over the last 800 years. They are used only during a coronation. Most of the time, they are kept at the tower of London carefully guarded by the

Yeoman of the Guard, also known as Beefeaters.[iii]

Like the crown jewels of England, I belong to Somebody. I am not my own. I am bought with a price. God values me and considers me His own property. As the psalmist says in Psalm 4:3, the Lord has set apart the godly for Himself.

As the Owner, God has the right to use me as He sees fit, whenever, wherever, and however He chooses. And since I am His personal property, He assumes full responsibility for my safety and well being. Not a Beefeater, but Yahweh Himself guards me and watches over me. I am under His protection. But it is up to me to keep the throne of my heart reserved for Him alone. He will not share me with another.

Most High God,

You have called me Your treasure. I am Yours and You are mine. Thank You that my worth and value are in You alone. You are all the protection I need. May my heart be kept pure for You alone. I am not my own. I am bought with a price. Help me to live like it today.

I Am A Member Of The Body

For even as the body is one and yet has many members,
and all the members of the body,
though they are many, are one body,
so also is Christ.
I Corinthians 12:12

For the body is not one member but many.
I Corinthians 12:14
Now you are Christ's body, and individually members of it. 1 1
Corinthians 12:27

I was attacked by a gas nozzle a while back. I dropped it on my right foot. Instantly my big toe notified me that it was part of my body. It was not a separate entity. My whole body commiserated with that big toe. As the fracture healed, that member of my body frequently reminded me that it was injured and needed special care.

In much the same way, the church is the body of Christ. We are members of one another. He is the head. We are the body. When one part suffers, the whole body suffers. We really do need each other. I cannot survive, much less thrive, without the rest of the body. And the body needs whatever gifting God has given me. I have a part to play. As I allow Him to, God places me in just the right place in His body. He knows where I am needed, where I can be most effective for Him. The One who knit me together in my mother's womb knows where I best fit. It is up to me to serve Him where I am, with all I am, for as long as He chooses.

Dear Lord Jesus,

You are the head. We are the body. Thank You for placing me just where You want me in the body and for gifting me in a unique way. Help me use all You have given me to build up other people and bring You the glory You alone deserve.

I Am A Warrior

Suffer hardship with me as a good soldier of Christ Jesus.
No soldier in active service entangles himself
in the affairs of everyday life,
so that he may please the one who enlisted him as a soldier.
II Timothy 2:3-4

One of the highest grossing media franchises of all time was the tv series Mission Impossible. The show featured special agents choosing to accept an extremely dangerous assignment. Once they accepted it, they had to be completely focused on their mission. Every episode began the same way, "Your mission should you choose to accept it is . . ."

Like those special agents, I was born into a war zone. But I did get to choose who I would serve. I chose to serve under the King of Kings. I willingly enlisted in His army. So I am bombarded by a spiritual enemy day after day. If I don't keep my shield up, some of his fiery darts will get through.

Jesus never promised I would make it through this fray without a scratch. The foe is brutal and he just keeps on coming. The danger is real. Souls hang in the balance. But I hold a blade that if rightly wielded, can tear down strongholds. And whatever things look like, I never fight alone. Although I may not be able to see them, there are more fighting for me than against me (II Kings 6:16-17). My Commanding Officer Himself holds me with His victorious right hand (Isaiah 41:10). And He promises that no weapon formed against me shall prosper (Isaiah 54:17). God has my back.

The mission is possible. But first I must choose to accept my assignment on a daily basis. When I live on mission and put myself completely at the disposal of my Commanding Officer, I am armed and dangerous. I am a warrior.

Commander of Hosts,
You are unbeatable. The battle is Yours. Thank You for allowing me to serve in Your army. Help me to stand in Your might and to take back what has been stolen from me. May I accept whatever mission

You have for me today. Give me grace to obey You. I put myself fully at Your disposal.

Fencing Lesson

Take your stance
And raise your sword,
Sharper than any
Forged by this world.
And as you say,
"En Garde!"
Look your opponent
In the eye,
Knowing full well,
Whose Name you bear.

Overcomer

She calls something
Out of nothing.
She sees past the veil
And hears the Spirit's whisper.
Often overlooked,
She is heard by heaven and hell.
Though her flesh may be frail,
She stands against the darkness.
She is armed and dangerous.
She is a prayer warrior.

Certain Outcome

Besieged, beaten down,
Often defeated,
Yet we triumph,
Wielding weapons of light,
Infused with the All-powerful,
Serving the Dragonslayer.

Teresa Burleson

I Am His Workmanship

For we are His workmanship,
created in Christ Jesus for good works,
which God prepared beforehand
so that we would walk in them.
Ephesians 2:10

Kintsugi (or kintsukuroi) means golden repair. It is a Japanese art form in which broken pieces of pottery are put back together using gold or some other precious metal instead of glue. The final product is more beautiful for having been broken.

I know what it feels like to be shattered. In a matter of weeks, my husband was dead from brain cancer. The one I looked to and depended on for 41 years, was suddenly gone. It was hard to go on. Sometimes I didn't know if I wanted to go on.

But the Master Craftsman showed up in the middle of my brokenness. Instead of worthless shards, He saw a work of art. Broken hearts are His specialty (Psalm 34:18).

And I can trust Him to be gentle with mine, because He, too, was crushed and put to grief (Isaiah 53:10). He is able to sympathize with my weakness (Heb. 4:15). As the KJV puts it, He is a High Priest who is touched with the feeling of my infirmities. According to Isaiah 53:3, He was a man of sorrows, acquainted with grief. So whenever I feel fragile like a broken reed (Isaiah 42:3), He comes not to break but to mend and restore. Whenever people or situations leave me broken and wounded, He comes to heal (Psalm 147:3). My Lord is the Master of kintsugi. He takes the fragments and makes me more beautiful for having been broken.

Mender of my soul,
I bring You all the broken pieces, all the wounded places in me. Thank You that You are trustworthy. You are infinitely patient and skilled. You know what You are doing. You will not waste my pain. Come and make me what You saw from the beginning.

Renewal

With such care,
One piece at a time,
We are glued together
By the Salvager of souls.
Give Him every bit
Of Your battered heart
And You will find
What He has created
And we have marred,
He can make anew.

Firsthand Knowledge

No stranger to grief,
This warrior still wears
The wounds we inflicted.
And because of us,
This God knows the feel
Of a broken heart.

Wing Binder

In a world that only takes,
You are the One who gives.
In a world where everyone shouts,
You are the One who listens.
In a world beset by storms,
You are the only Shelter.
In a world that smashes
So many dreams,
You are the One
Who binds the broken wing.

Stained Glass

Nothing is discarded
Or forgotten.
Every jagged piece
Of our lives
That is put
In that skillful hand,
Is joined to the whole
In just the place
It was made to fill.
And when He is through,
Each broken piece
Shall catch the Light
And reflect the One
Who is
Unquenchable Fire.

I Am A Runner

Therefore since we have
so great a cloud of witnesses surrounding us,
let us also lay aside every encumbrance
and the sin which so easily entangles us,
and let us run with endurance the race that is set before us.
Hebrews 12:1

The hare should have won. In Aesop's beloved fable, *The Tortoise and the Hare*, he is in the lead. And he has every natural advantage. With their long hind legs, hares can cover as much as 50 mph for short distances. But he grows cocky and loses focus. He decides to take a siesta. The tortoise just keeps plodding along and wins the race.

Like the tortoise, I have short legs. I was not built for speed. Although I have never competed in the natural, I am in a cross-country marathon of a different sort. It is the race Jesus has called me to.

He has gone before me and made a way. But every day I choose whether I will follow.

The stakes are high and the prize is real. It does matter for all eternity whether I reach the finish line. He is watching and He cheers for me.

But three things are necessary if I really want to win. I must let go of anything that holds me back. I must stay focused on the goal. And I must endure or keep on keeping on in His power. I want to not only run well, but to finish well. Many have begun well but then disqualified themselves before they reached the finish line (I Cor. 9:24-25).

What can pick me up and keep me going on the days (and there are many) when I feel like I can't go another step? What about when I wonder if it's really worth it? Why keep on running anyway? There is really only one reason. He Himself is the prize. He alone is worthy. So today I will fix my eyes on the One who left it all behind for my sake. I will follow after Him.

Dear Jesus,

You are my Trailblazer. You are worthy. You are worth it all. Thank You that You are watching. You are cheering for me. You are my reason to run. Help me to run well this day. Help me to finish well.

Teresa Burleson

The Long Distance Runner

Weary, so weary

Of this cross country marathon,

The runner stumbles.

There she lies,

Unable to get up.

Then Lifegiver breathes

Into the burning lungs,

Into the aching

Tendons and sinews.

Power from on high

Falls on the runner.

And once again,

She stands.

Remembering the Forerunner,

Who is reason enough to run,

Who is watching,

Who cheers for her,

She is undeterred.

She will finish

The race she is given.

I Am His Dwelling Place

Do you not know that you are a temple of God
and that the Spirit of God dwells in you?
I Corinthians 3:16

I am a fixer upper. From the foundation to the rafters, this heart needs to be restored. Totally. I would be condemned except the Owner of all chooses to reside in me. Not satisfied with a visit every now and then, He desires to make me His dwelling place.

But how do I respond? Am I looking for just a quick visit or do I want to be indwelt? Am I willing to welcome Him into every part of my life? The front door only opens from the inside. God is a Gentleman and He will not force His way in. But every time I hear His knock and open the door, He will come in and fellowship (Rev. 3:20). Only there in His Presence, do I find fullness of joy (Psalm 16:11).

And if while the Lord is here, He should want to make repairs or do some remodeling, may I be quick to say yes. He is the Owner after all. His hand drew the blueprint. He is the Master Builder. And He can be trusted to complete what He has started in me (Phil 1:6). Whatever it takes, this Builder can make even a junk heap into a house fit for such a King.

Master Builder,
Come into all the rooms of my heart and have Your way. Thank You that You know what You're doing. Thank You that You will complete the good work You have begun in me.

Indwelt

He still chooses
Condemned buildings
For His residence.
Morning by morning
He is still ready
To renovate
Until this hovel
Is made a palace
Fit for the Owner.

Teresa Burleson

I Am A Worshipper

But an hour is coming and now is,
when the true worshippers will worship the Father
in spirit and truth;
for such people the Father seeks to be His worshippers.
God is spirit and those who worship Him
must worship in spirit and truth.
John 4:23-24

When an angel comes to call, grown men cower at the sight. Upon seeing one roll away the stone, the guards at the tomb quaked and fell down like dead. So I can't imagine what the prophet Isaiah felt as he was taken up into the throne room and saw for himself the One who is consuming fire (Heb. 12:29). He beheld the King of Kings in his glory (Is. 6:1-7). The six-winged seraphim surrounding the Lord cried out, "Holy, Holy, Holy". Seeing the Light unmixed with any darkness, Isaiah was shaken to the core, sickened by his own uncleanness and unworthiness. But a seraphim touched his lips with a live coal from the altar and reassured him that his sin was forgiven.

Like Isaiah, I may hesitate to approach the One who exposes all my vileness and unworthiness. But because my sins are forgiven for all time, I can enter His presence not with dread, but with delight.

I am made to worship. It is in my DNA. I will worship someone or something whether I realize it or not. And little by little, I will become like what I worship. Mine is the privilege of worshipping the One True God. He doesn't need my worship. Far from it. But I need to be reminded that He alone is God and I am not. When I worship Him in Spirit and in Truth, the Lord pours His worth into my unworthiness. As I celebrate who He really is, He shows Himself God in my life. Then He can make me clean and whole. He restores me. Beholding His face, I become a little more like Him. Today I will adore Him just because He is God. And I will never be the same.

God Most High,

You alone are worthy. You alone can satisfy the deepest part of me. May I enter Your courts with thanksgiving and make You my highest joy. May I see You as You are. Thank You for being such an awesome God. Thank You that You are big enough to worship.

Invocation

Without You,
We languish.
We wither and die.
Apart from You,
We are but dust.
Come Fire of God.
Come Wind of God.
Come Three-In-One.
Oh, breathe life
Into each waiting heart.
Inhabit Your people.
And these dead bones
Shall once more dance.

Inner Court

This place is holy
Because You are here.
You see how vile I am.
Yet here is where
You take
All that I am,
All that I am not,
And in exchange,
You give me Yourself.
Here Omnipotence
And utter weakness
Intersect.
You meet me here
In this most holy place.

Teresa Burleson

High And Lifted Up

(Isaiah 6:1-7)
All pride,
All pretense
Lie shattered
By the Light,
Inescapable Light.
Now I see Him
As He is.
And next to Him,
I see
My filthiness,
My nothingness.
Yet He is Mercy.
Fire from the altar
Brushes these sinful lips.
I am purged.
I am sent.
I am His mouthpiece.
And along with
Six-winged seraphim,
All I can do
Is cry out,
"Holy! Holy! Holy!"

I Am His Bride

For I am jealous for you with a godly jealousy;
for I betrothed you to one husband,
so that to Christ I might present you as a pure virgin.
II Corinthians 11:2

In 1936, Edward VIII became the first British monarch to willingly abdicate. He was Prince of Wales, the future King of England. But he gave up the throne in order to marry Wallis Simpson, the woman he loved. Jesus gave up far, far more to win His bride. He left His godhood behind and became one of us.

Marriage symbolizes the kind of love Christ has for His bride, the church. We are His betrothed (Hosea 2:19-20). He wants to share eternity with us. He desires us to be where He is so we can share His glory (John 17:24), and so we can rule and reign with Him.

A husband and wife enter into a covenant to belong to each other exclusively for life. In the same way, my Heavenly Bridegroom deserves no less than my first love (Rev. 2:4), not second, third, fourth, or fifth place in my heart. He will brook no rivals. He is worthy of my single-hearted devotion. Even now He is preparing a place for us (John 14:2-3). And He is making us a pure and spotless bride ready for our wedding day (Ephesians 5:25-27). It will be a day like no other. And I have a place at the table.

Heavenly Bridegroom,
You alone are worthy. You see how many temptations, how many distractions there are in this life. You see how prone I am to leave my first love. Rekindle the flame of devotion in me, wherever I have grown cold. Help me to love You with my whole heart. Thank You that You are coming back to receive us unto Yourself. Thank You that I will see You as You are and I will be like You.

The Betrothed

Though she has never
Seen His face,
His favor is
Her sun, her breath,
Her drink, her bread.
He has never stopped seeking her.
There is nothing
He has not given
To make her His.
And when at last
She beholds Him
As He is,
She shall no longer
Wear filthy rags
Or shrink back in shame,
This glorious,
Blood-bought princess bride.

Bridegroom

Earth wears a gown
Of sun-spangled green.
See how she is arrayed
For the One and Only.
He has paid the price
And won the bride.
He is coming
To claim what is His.
And every Spring
Is but a dress rehearsal
For His nuptial day
When we will behold
The Rightfully Adored.

I Am His Witness

*But you will receive power
when the Holy Spirit has come upon you
and you shall be my witnesses
both in Jerusalem and in all Judea and Samaria,
and even to the remotest part of the earth.*
Acts 1:8

Sometimes called "the Billy Graham of India," E. Stanley Jones was a well-known American missionary, evangelist, and author. He preached in almost every country of the world. But his first sermon was a flop. Although he prepared for 3 weeks, it did not go well. He ended up sitting down in shame and confusion. But something inside told him to stand back up and just tell the congregation what Christ had done in his life. As a result, a young man was saved. What E. Stanley Jones learned was that God did not need a lawyer to argue for Him. He simply wanted a witness. As he later wrote, his job was to tell what Grace had done for an unworthy life.[iv]

When an eyewitness testifies, the Judge and jury listen. Such a testimony can be irrefutable. The Apostle John wrote about being an eyewitness in I John 1:1-3. For three years, he literally saw, heard, and touched the Son of God. Although I have not had the privilege of knowing Him in the flesh, like John did, I, too, am a witness. Fifty years ago, I first accepted Jesus as Lord and Savior. And I can testify to all He has done in that 50 years. He has brought me out of the darkness into the Light. He called me to write, kept me from marrying the wrong man, and brought the right man into my life. He gave us two children by adoption and blessed me with three grandchildren. And now He is my solace in the midst of widowhood. I am His witness. May I ever be ready to share what He has done in my life.

Lord Jesus,
  Thank You that You don't need anyone to be

Your lawyer. May I never trivialize or be ashamed of the testimony You have given me. Thank You for all You have done in my life. Help me to be ready to share it with others.

Teresa Burleson

I Am An Heir

*The Spirit Himself testifies with our spirit
that we are children of God, and if children, heirs also,
heirs of God and fellow heirs with Christ,
if indeed we suffer with Him,
so that we may also be glorified with Him.*
Romans 8:16-17

The land was theirs for the taking. Exactly 40 years to the day, after they left Egypt, the Israelites finally reached the Jordan. It was time to cross over. They were about to celebrate their first Passover in the Promised Land. Canaan was their inheritance. God was faithful to bring them in and kept every promise. But they had a part to play. They had to enter in and occupy or possess all the territory God gave them. God said it was theirs. But they had to believe the Lord enough to conquer the Canaanites and take what was theirs.

Like the Israelites, I have an inheritance. I am a

co-heir with Christ. An incorruptible inheritance awaits me in heaven (I Peter 1:4). But what about all He has for me in this life? According to Dr. Everek R. Storms of Ontario, who actually counted them, there are 8,810 promises in the Bible. Of those, 7,487 are from God to man.[v]

They are my promised land (II Peter 1:4). And they cover everything I could possibly need. But how many have I actually claimed by faith and made my own? I have wandered in the barren wilderness long enough. It is high time for me to start taking the land, to enter into all that God has said I can have.

Exactly how do I inherit the promises? In Heb. 6:12, I am told it takes faith and patience. There will be stiff resistance. Satan is a squatter and he does not leave willingly. It is up to me to enforce his eviction in the All-Powerful Name of Jesus.

Heavenly Father,

Thank You for all You have given me and made available to me in Christ Jesus. Give me the faith to take You at Your Word. You are the Promise Keeper. Help me to appropriate Your promises and make them my own. Thank You for the unfading inheritance that is waiting for me in Heaven.

Teresa Burleson

I Am More Than A Conqueror

Yet in all these things we are more than conquerors through Him who loved us.
Romans 8:37 NKJV

Some called it impossible. No one had ever done it. Then in 1954, Roger Bannister, an Oxford medical student, broke the 4-minute mile. He proved it was possible. His breakthrough paved the way for many others. Since then over 500 American men have beaten his record.

In a much greater way, Jesus blazed the path for me. He turned the greatest tragedy into the ultimate triumph. He took back all the usurper stole. He proved He is the Resurrection and the Life by coming out of the tomb. This is not just some hope for the distant future, but the present reality. It can be my reality if I choose to believe. Because I am

His and He is mine, His victory is my victory. His resurrection power resides in me. In John 16:33, Jesus assures me that He has overcome the world. I have His Word on it. Present circumstances are nothing compared with death being defanged once and for all. The battle is won. Because Jesus in the undefeated, all things are possible (Matt. 19:26). So, yes, I am an overcomer. I simply have to take Him at His Word.

Dear Lord Jesus,

You are the Risen and Victorious One. Every knee shall bow and every tongue confess that You are Lord to the glory of God the Father. You broke every chain. You broke the curse. You have overcome the world. Thank You for living inside me. Thank You that I can overcome in Your Name.

The Undefeated

What love held You there
On that Friday
When midnight came at noon?

What blood joined God and man
As they were
In the garden?

What power loosed You
On that Sunday
When death met His Master?

The Victor

Shepherd still seeking the stray.
Zeal cleansing the temple.
Forgiveness lifting the fallen,
Tender shoot breaking death asunder,
Victor for all time.

Teresa Burleson

Acknowledgments

I would like to thank the following journals for their publication of the following poems:

"Indwelt" appeared in *Time of Singing*.

"The Victor" appeared in *Catechumenate*.

"The Vinedresser" appeared in *Catechumenate*.

"Metamorphosis" appeared in *Smile and Mature Years*.

"Expose" appeared in *Evangel*.

"The Undefeated" appeared in *Emmanuel*.

"A Fierce Embrace" appeared in the anthology *Bigger Than Me* by Oprelle Publications

"Overcomer" appeared in *Silver Wings* and *The Breakthrough Intercessor*.

"Gomer Speaks," "Passover," "Image Bearer," and "A Fierce Embrace" appeared in the online publication *Agape Review*.

"Metamorphosis" appeared in the online publication *Highland Park Poetry/The Muses Gallery*.

"Child of the Father," "The Craftsman," "Relationship," "The Vinedresser," "The Alternative," "Certain Outcome," "Wing Binder," and "Renewal," appeared in my book entitle *The Pilgrim's Lyre* published by AuthorHouse.

"Metamorphosis," and "Firsthand Knowledge," appeared in my chapbook entitled *Rose Without Thorns* published by Finishing Line Press.

"Stained Glass" appeared in *Alive Now* and *The Vision*.

Notes

[i] Walter B. Knight, Knight's Master Book of New Illustration (Grand Rapids, 1981), p.324.

[ii] "Titanic," Wikipedia, n. d. https://www.bing.com (3/12/22).

[iii] "Crown Jewels of the United Kingdom," Wikipedia, n.d., https:// enwikipedia.org/wiki/Crown-Jewels-of-the- United-Kingdom (3/12/22).

[iv] Robert J. Morgan, Preacher's Source Book of Creative Sermon Illustration (Nashville, 2007), p.645.

[v] Ibid., p. 282.

Made in the USA
Monee, IL
27 August 2023

41577781R00069